WITHDRAWN

OCT _ 2002

DATE DUE

Yellowstone
National Park

by Mike Graf

Reading Consultant:
Dr. Robert Miller
Professor of Special Education
Minnesota State University, Mankato

Bridgestone Books
an imprint of Capstone Press
Mankato, Minnesota

Bridgestone Books are published by Capstone Press
151 Good Counsel Drive, P.O. Box 669, Mankato, Minnesota 56002
http://www.capstone-press.com

Library of Congress Cataloging-in-Publication Data
Graf, Mike.
    Yellowstone National Park / by Mike Graf.
    v. cm.—(National parks)
    Includes bibliographical references and index.
    Contents: Introduction—How yellowstone formed—People in yellowstone—Animals—
Plants—Weather—Activities—Safety—Park issues—Map activity—About national parks—
Words to know—Read more—Useful addresses—Internet sites.
    ISBN 0-7368-1379-9 (hardcover)
    1. Yellowstone National Park—Juvenile literature. [1. Yellowstone National Park.
2. National parks and reserves.] I. Title. II. National parks (Mankato, Minn.)
F722 .G73 2003
917.87'52–dc21   2001008096

Editorial Credits
Blake A. Hoena, editor; Karen Risch, product planning editor; Linda Clavel, designer;
    Anne McMullen, illustrator; Alta Schaffer, photo researcher

Photo Credits
Ben R. Frakes/Houserstock, 12
Beth Davidow, 14, 16, 18
Bruce Jackson/Gnass Photo Images, 4
Digital Vision, 1
Doranne Jacobson, 17
Jeff Henry/Roche Jaune Pictures, Inc., cover, 6, 8
Mark & Sue Werner/The Image Finders, 10

1 2 3 4 5 6 07 06 05 04 03 02

Table of Contents

Montana

Idaho Wyoming

4

Yellowstone National Park

Yellowstone National Park lies mostly in Wyoming. But it also extends into Montana and Idaho. The park covers almost 3,500 square miles (9,070 square kilometers) of land. More than 3 million people visit Yellowstone each year.

The U.S. government creates national parks to protect unique natural areas. This idea actually began with Yellowstone. Early explorers marveled at Yellowstone's scenic beauty. They thought the area should be preserved for others to see. In 1872, the U.S. government set aside land for Yellowstone National Park.

Yellowstone is known for its many thermal features. The park has geysers, steam vents, hot springs, and boiling mud volcanoes. Old Faithful is the most famous geyser in the park. For more than 100 years this geyser has erupted every 45 to 120 minutes. It shoots out a shower of steam and water about 200 feet (60 meters) high.

Lower Yellowstone Falls is one of the many features visitors can see in Yellowstone.

How Yellowstone Formed

Yellowstone was created by volcanic eruptions. As many as three eruptions happened in the area. The last occurred about 600,000 years ago. The eruptions left behind a giant caldera. A caldera is a collapsed volcano.

Earth's crust is thin in the caldera. In most areas, Earth's crust is 20 miles (32 kilometers) thick. It is about 2 miles (3.2 kilometers) thick in the caldera. The thin crust causes many of the park's thermal features.

Magma, or melted rock, lies under Earth's crust. Thermal features form when water from snow or rain runs down through cracks in the crust. The magma then heats this water. Water increases in size when heated. This action creates pressure. The hot water then pushes up through the cracks to release the pressure. The escaping pressure causes geysers to erupt and hot springs to boil.

Boiling mud volcanoes are one type of thermal feature in Yellowstone.

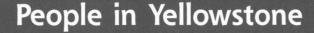

People in Yellowstone

American Indians have lived in the Yellowstone area for more than 10,000 years. The Minnetaree Indians called Yellowstone "Mi tsi a-da-zi," which means "Rock Yellow River." Some of the rocks and soil in Yellowstone have a yellow color. American Indians in the area hunted bison and gathered obsidian. They used this dark volcanic glass to make arrowheads.

John Colter is known as the first white man to see the Yellowstone area. In the early 1800s, he trapped beavers along the Yellowstone River. He first described the area as being full of "hidden fires, smoking pits, and [harmful] steams." Many people did not believe his stories of Yellowstone.

In the mid-1800s, explorers started to travel to Yellowstone. They wanted to know if Colter's stories were true. After seeing Yellowstone, these people helped convince the U.S. government to preserve the area.

American Indians built shelters from trees in the Yellowstone area.

Animals

Yellowstone's most famous animals are bears. Black bears and grizzly bears live throughout most of Yellowstone. The park is one of the only places in the lower 48 states where grizzlies still live.

Many herd animals live in the park. About 20,000 elk live in Yellowstone. This herd is the largest elk herd anywhere in the world. About 3,000 bison live in Yellowstone. Moose also live in the park. People often see them near water. Bighorn sheep are common in high, rocky areas. Pronghorn antelope graze in the park's northern areas. This animal is North America's fastest mammal. It can run up to 60 miles (97 kilometers) per hour.

Many other animals live in the park. Predators such as coyotes, mountain lions, and wolves hunt other park animals for food. Yellowstone also has mule deer, beavers, and badgers. Birds such as bald eagles, trumpeter swans, and pelicans nest in the park.

Mountain lions are one type of predator that lives in Yellowstone.

Plants

Several types of trees grow in Yellowstone. Lodgepole pines are the most common. American Indians used these tall, straight trees to build their homes. Douglas fir, spruce, whitebark pine, and cottonwood trees also grow in the park.

The northern end of the park is dry. In this area, fields of sagebrush and forests of aspen trees grow.

Yellowstone's high mountains are an alpine tundra, or frozen grassy area. Mosses, lichens, wildflowers, and small shrubs grow in this area.

In the summer of 1988, large forest fires swept through Yellowstone. They burned almost one-third of the park's land. People once thought that forest fires were harmful. But after these fires, new grasses and wildflowers started to grow. The fires' heat also caused seeds from pinecones to open and sprout into new trees. In this way, natural forest fires can be helpful to plant life.

New wildflowers have grown where fires destroyed forests in Yellowstone.

Weather

Yellowstone has four seasons. Most people visit the park in summer because the weather is pleasant. Summer temperatures usually range from 70 to 85 degrees Fahrenheit (21 to 29 degrees Celsius). But the nights can be cool. Thunderstorms are common in the summer.

Temperatures in fall are cooler than summer temperatures. At night, temperatures may be below freezing. Snow can start to fall in late September.

Yellowstone's winter is very cold. Day temperatures may range from 0 to 20 degrees Fahrenheit (minus 18 to minus 7 degrees Celsius). The park is covered in snow during winter and many of the park's roads are closed.

Spring can be cold and snowy. The nights often are below freezing. Around May, the snow begins to melt. Water from the melting snow overflows the park's lakes and rivers.

Snow covers Yellowstone during the winter.

Yellowstone has many activities for people to do. People can hike or ride horseback. The park has more than 1,000 miles (1,600 kilometers) of trails.

Many people sightsee at Yellowstone. They like to view Yellowstone's wildlife. Lamar Valley is the most popular area for this activity. Visitors also come to see Yellowstone's many thermal features.

People enjoy many water activities in Yellowstone. They fish in the park's rivers and lakes. People also can take boat rides.

People need to be careful while hiking in Yellowstone. The water in thermal features is very hot. The ground near them may be thin and breakable. People have been burned by Yellowstone's hot waters. Park visitors should stay on pathways while hiking near thermal features.

In spring, the park's rivers and waterfalls overflow with melting snow. People need to be careful while hiking near these waterways. The rushing waters could carry them downstream.

Park Issues

Several problems concern officials at Yellowstone. In the past, bison that left the park to search for food during winter were shot. Officials were concerned that these bison would spread diseases to nearby cattle herds. Recently, park officials completed a plan to allow some bison to migrate out of the park.

In the early 1900s, wolves were poisoned or shot. But today, park officials are working to restore the wolf population. Wolves hunt other animals for food. They help keep animal populations from growing too large. Park workers have moved wolves from Canada to the park. More than 150 wolves now live in Yellowstone.

People ride snowmobiles in the park during winter. In recent years, this activity has become very popular. Park officials are concerned that snowmobiles will hurt or frighten animals. Officials want to reduce the number of snowmobiles in the park, or ban them completely.

Bison sometimes leave the park during winter as they search for food.

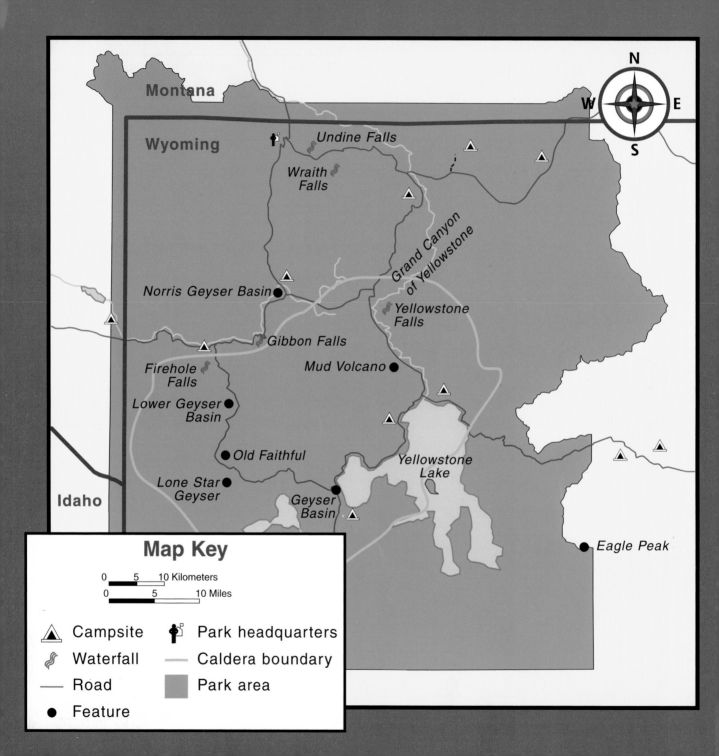

Map Key

0   5   10 Kilometers

0   5   10 Miles

△ Campsite

⚕ Waterfall

— Road

● Feature

⚐ Park headquarters

— Caldera boundary

    Park area

Montana

Wyoming

Undine Falls

Wraith Falls

Grand Canyon of Yellowstone

Norris Geyser Basin ●

Yellowstone Falls

Gibbon Falls

Firehole Falls

Mud Volcano ●

Lower Geyser ● Basin

● Old Faithful

Lone Star ● Geyser

Geyser Basin

Yellowstone Lake

Idaho

● Eagle Peak

N
W   E
S

Map Activity

Yellowstone National Park has many interesting features for visitors to see. Plan a trip by finding sights that you would like to see in the park.

What You Need
Ruler

What You Do
1. Find the symbol of a campsite in the map's key. Then find a campsite on the map.
2. Pick sights that you would like to see. You can find out how far they are from your campsite by using the ruler and the scale in the map's key.

Possible Sights to See
1. Yellowstone has many mountain peaks. At 11,358 feet (3,462 meters) above sea level, Eagle Peak is the tallest.
2. The Grand Canyon of Yellowstone contains the Yellowstone River and Yellowstone Falls.
3. Yellowstone Lake is North America's largest mountain lake.
4. Yellowstone has more than 10,000 thermal features, including geysers and mud volcanoes.

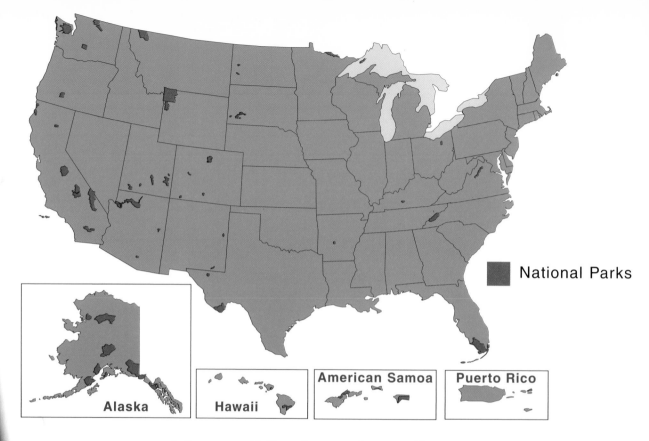

National Parks

Alaska

Hawaii

American Samoa

Puerto Rico

About National Parks

In 1872, the U.S. government set aside land for Yellowstone National Park. Lawmakers wanted to protect this area so that people could enjoy its sights. Yellowstone was the first U.S. national park. It also was the first national park in the world.

Today, the National Park Service runs more than 50 national parks. These parks protect unique natural areas. People cannot hunt or build on park lands. But they can camp, hike, and view the scenery of these areas.

Words to Know

alpine (AL-pine)—relating to mountains

caldera (kal-DUR-uh)—a collapsed volcano

erupt (i-RUHPT)—to shoot out with great force; water and steam shoot out of geysers.

lichen (LYE-ken)—a mosslike growth on rocks and trees

magma (MAG-muh)—melted rock that is found beneath Earth's crust

migrate (MYE-grate)—to move from one area to another

obsidian (ob-SI-dee-en)—a dark glass formed by cooling volcanic lava

preserve (pri-ZURV)—to keep something in its original state

sea level (SEE LEV-uhl)—the average surface level of the world's oceans

tundra (TUHN-druh)—a frozen, treeless area

unique (yoo-NEEK)—one of a kind

Read More

Meister, Cari. *Yellowstone National Park.* Going Places. Minneapolis: Abdo & Daughters, 2000.

Petersen, David. *Yellowstone National Park.* A True Book. New York: Children's Press, 2001.

Raatma, Lucia. *Our National Parks.* Let's See. Minneapolis: Compass Point Books, 2002.

Useful Addresses

National Park Service
1849 C Street NW
Washington, DC 20240

Yellowstone National Park
Information Office
PO Box 168
Yellowstone National Park,
WY 82190

Internet Sites

National Park Service—Yellowstone National Park
http://www.nps.gov/yell
The Total Yellowstone Page—Yellowstone National Park
http://www.yellowstone-natl-park.com
Yellowstone National Park—Just for Kids
http://www.nps.gov/yell/kidstuff

Index